EXCAVATING THE PAST

MESA VERDE

Mary Quigley

Heinemann Library
Chicago, Illinois

INTRODUCTION

Long ago, there were no people in North or South America. Then, about 20,000 to 35,000 years ago, people migrated on foot across a bridge of land and ice that spanned the gap between Asia and Alaska. They were able to do this because much of the ocean water was frozen in huge glaciers. The sea level dropped and the edges of the oceans drew back, exposing land. The land bridge that formed crossed the Bering Strait and allowed humans to cross over to North and South America.

The people who first came to North America found a much different place than the one we know today. This fertile area was filled with large mammoths, mastodons, sloths, saber-tooth cats, and bears. The people were hunter-gatherers. They ate the animals they hunted and plants that they gathered.

Life as hunter-gatherers meant constantly moving. They traveled on foot in small groups, following herds of migrating animals and searching for edible plants. For shelter they used trees and caves. To stay warm, they wore furs from the animals that they hunted. They moved according to climate, season, and food supply. Their progress was slow, and over many generations they learned to adapt to each climate and habitat.

Fantasy or Fact?

Although most people believe that the first humans to reach North America came across the Bering Strait land bridge, there are other theories. Radiocarbon dating is making scientists wonder whether there were humans in North America much earlier than they thought. If so, the land bridge might not have been available to use. Perhaps they used boats instead and crossed the Atlantic Ocean from Europe or the Pacific Ocean from Asia. Many scientists are investigating these new theories.

▷ *Mesa Verde has amazed archaeologists for decades.*

WHO WERE The Anasazi?

You may have heard the name "Anasazi" used for the culture at Mesa Verde. Anasazi is a Navajo word that can mean "ancient ones." It has also been interpreted to mean "enemy people." Because of that, we now refer to them as Ancestral Puebloans instead. This also is a better name because it reminds us of the connection between the Pueblo people of today and the ancient people of the Mesa Verde area.

Ancestral Puebloans and culture

Some of the first Puebloan people found their way to the Four Corners area of North America. It is called this because it is where corners of Utah, Colorado, Arizona, and New Mexico meet. In this area are many mesas, which are flat plateaus with steep sides and moist, fertile land on the top. One large mesa was called "Mesa Verde," which means "green table."

Though they had been nomadic people who traveled in a constant search for food, the lush mesa tops offered prime land for agriculture and they learned to farm. Farming meant that their lifestyle changed drastically. Rather than being constantly on the move, they settled down and built towns. We call the people who settled here around C.E. 550 the Anasazi or Ancestral Puebloans. Archaeologists divide the Ancestral Puebloan culture into periods that are defined by artistic, religious, technological, and social advances.

▷ *This map shows the land bridge that may have been used to cross into the Americas.*

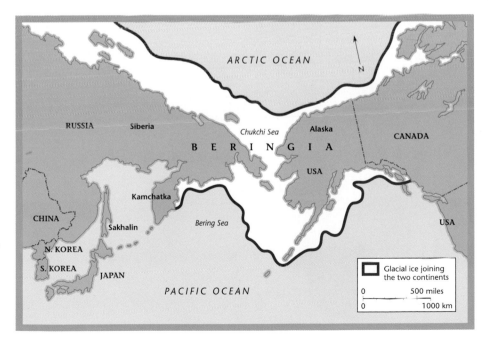

The Basketmakers

Before arriving at Mesa Verde, the Ancestral Puebloans are known by historians as the Basketmakers. This is because some of the main evidence of their culture is the baskets they made. For people on the move, basketmaking was an important skill. By weaving plant materials into vessels, they could carry the food that they gathered. Archaeologists learn about how the baskets were made, and what they were used for, by studying baskets that have been found at Mesa Verde. Around C.E. 550, the Ancestral Puebloans brought their culture to the Mesa Verde region.

When the Ancestral Puebloans arrived at Mesa Verde, the people settled in small villages. They were replacing their nomadic lifestyle by building permanent homes. They also began to learn how to make pottery. Making pottery suited their new lifestyle now that carrying heavy breakable pots was not an issue. They introduced beans to their diet, which were very nourishing. They used simple tools to create farms on the mesa top.

◁ *The Ancestral Puebloans made very distinctive pottery. Many artifacts, like these water carriers, have been found in one piece at Mesa Verde.*

Archaeology Challenge

How do we know how many people lived at Mesa Verde at a given time? The dwellings give clues. Archaeologists can estimate how many people could live in a dwelling and multiply that by the number of dwellings. Mesa Verde has generated population estimates ranging from 5,000 to 30,000.

Pueblos

By about C.E. 750 the Ancestral Puebloans began to improve their houses. They made pueblo dwellings of wooden posts and sun-dried mud. Within about 250 years they were cutting sandstone into blocks to build multi-room complexes with spaces for cooking, sleeping, and storing food.

The Classic period

The Classic or Great Pueblo period lasted from C.E. 1100 to C.E. 1300. By then Mesa Verde had become a civilization that survived through cooperation. They divided the responsibilities among members of the community, specialized in certain work based on their skills and customs, and traded by bartering. They further developed their creative and religious expression through art and ceremony. Their settlement shows evidence that a space was made for gathering together. In this setting they could make political decisions, practice their religion, and socialize. It was during this period that they moved into the caves in the cliffs.

▷ *The Ancestral Puebloans managed to grow crops on the mesa tops.*

Life in the cliffs

The Ancestral Puebloan people managed to build a stable year-round community with a thriving culture, despite the dry desert summers and bitter winters. They still were able to grow crops and build homes using natural materials, their own hands, and simple tools. They found opportunities for play and for worship. They studied the stars, and learned to craft beautiful pottery, jewelry, and woven items. They left images on stones that tell a part of their story. Today you can visit their deserted villages. You can also try to figure out why, suddenly, around C.E. 1300 the people of Mesa Verde left. Where did they go? And why?

▽ *The Ancestral Puebloans changed their hunter-gatherer lifestyle to a more settled one at Mesa Verde.*

Ancestral Puebloan finds

It takes many people to accurately document the story of a culture. Archaeologists look for things that early people left behind, such as dwellings, clothing, pottery, baskets, rock paintings, and etchings—even skeletal remains. But to understand the meaning of what they find, they work with specialists. For instance medical doctors can help them to know how old someone lived by looking at the skeleton. A geologist, who studies Earth and its rocks, can help determine where the clay in a particular pot came from. This may tell where the person migrated from or whether they traded with someone from another region for their pottery. Anthropologists and linguists add their knowledge of stories and languages.

Archaeology Challenge

Spear points are one kind of artifact that is studied to determine when humans first came to North America. Sometimes the style of the point gives archaeologists an idea of the time period in which it was made. Used alone this method may be misleading since spear points were often damaged or re-sharpened after use and took on a new look. But, when spear points are found with other artifacts, such as mammoth bones, the age of all the items can be assumed to be fairly close. Living creatures have carbon in their bones and radiocarbon dating can determine their age fairly accurately.

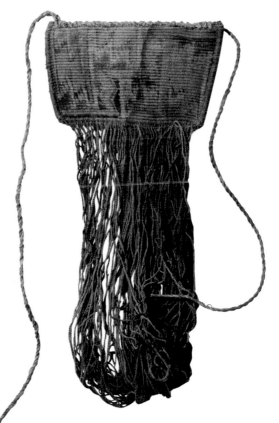

△ *The Ancestral Puebloans wove clothing and baskets out of plant fibers.*

EARLY DISCOVERIES

The Mesa Verde region is the perfect place for learning about people of the past by using archaeology. The dry climate keeps artifacts from rotting and molding. The remote clifftop location prevents them from being washed away, lost, or broken. Wood-chewing insects find the area too dry to live in. Mesa Verde holds treasures, such as split willow baskets and clay pottery with painted designs. Archaeologists have even found fur clothing made from hide and cloth, jewelry, and tools. Every item tells a part of the story of the Ancestral Puebloan people.

Archaeologists have been helped by the fact that nobody moved into the Mesa Verde cliff dwellings after the Ancestral Puebloans moved away. Everything was left unchanged and undisturbed. Native people from surrounding areas respected the people who had lived there before and left their homes alone. Also, while the Ancestral Puebloans had learned how to farm and live in that region, it was difficult land that did not appeal to settlers. Although occasionally a traveler may have encountered some of the dwellings of Mesa Verde, European settlers were not widely aware of most of the Mesa Verde villages until the late 1800s.

▷ *The dwellings were first spotted from across the ravine.*

The discovery of Cliff Palace

Richard Wetherill and his brother-in-law Charles Mason were raising cattle in the 1800s. They had become friends with the Native Americans of the area. Richard was a Quaker with a reputation for being peaceful. He had learned some of the Ute language. His family had earned the trust of their Native American neighbors. Because of this friendship, they were allowed to let their cattle wander on the grassy land near the abandoned Mesa Verde settlement. As they became familiar with the land, they found a few small, scattered cliff dwellings. Other people had stumbled upon scattered pueblo houses as well. Then, one day, a Ute chief named Acowitz told Wetherill a story of an amazing place—the home of "the Ancient Ones." But he said it would be wrong to take him there.

△ *Spruce Tree House was an exciting find.*

In December 1888 when Wetherill and Mason were searching for lost cattle, he found himself looking across a ravine at what came to be known as Cliff Palace. It looked like a city with several hundred rooms built into a mountain. He had accidentally discovered some of the most dramatic architecture at Mesa Verde. It was the very place that the Ute chief had spoken of. Richard and his family found many other Ancestral Puebloan buildings after that, including Spruce Tree House.

▷ *Axe heads are one of the types of tools found at Mesa Verde.*

Excavating

After their discovery, cattle ranching did not interest Wetherill and Mason nearly as much as their new fascination with archaeology. But Richard Wetherill was not a professional archaeologist. In fact he had little formal schooling. But he asked questions, got help, and learned as he went. Wetherill and his brothers began to search for artifacts and tried to piece together the story of the Ancestral Puebloans. Many people have criticized the work of the Wetherills because they sold artifacts and carved their initials into the abandoned dwellings that they found. But others have defended their work by pointing out that archaeology was a newly emerging science, and what they did was accepted practice at the time.

Archaeology Challenge

One of the Wetherills' most amazing finds was a mummy that was buried in a large 5 foot (1.5 meter) basket with a blanket of canary and bluebird feathers. They named her "The Princess" because of the exceptional care that went into her burial. They also found other human remains. But these remains create a problem for archaeologists. While they can learn a lot about how people lived by studying skeletons and mummies, there are some serious ethical concerns about the practice of excavating and analyzing them. For the descendants of these human beings, archaeological study can seem like grave robbing. It can also be disturbing to them on a spiritual level. To be more sensitive, in some cases human remains are now being removed from museums and returned to their burial places.

◁ Care was taken to preserve decorated objects such as this painted pottery. Archaeologists were lucky to find so many complete pieces at Mesa Verde.

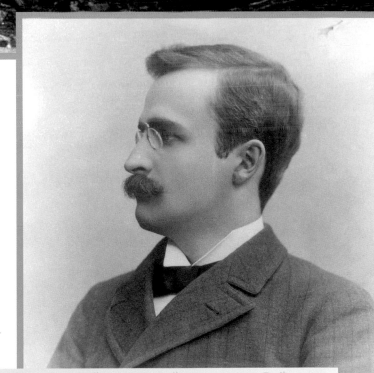

△ *Richard Wetherill triggered the interest of many others by publicizing Mesa Verde.*

▷ *Gustaf Nordenskiöld was one of the first excavators at Mesa Verde.*

Mesa Verde becomes famous

News of the Wetherill's discovery brought many people to Mesa Verde. Some were happy just to look, but others stole artifacts. Many things were accidentally damaged.

Gustaf Nordenskiöld was a Swede who came to the American west looking for a climate that would help him to treat his tuberculosis. He had visited digs before and Richard Wetherill asked for his help at Mesa Verde in 1891. Nordenskiöld helped Wetherill to study, document, and

△ *Richard and Al Wetherill looking for artifacts.*

preserve the artifacts. They worked well together. Nordenskiöld was clever and educated and Wetherill knew a lot about the local area and was very enthusiastic about the project.

Nordenskiöld discovered a great deal about the Ancestral Puebloan culture, but he was also criticized for taking artifacts from Mesa Verde to exhibit in a museum in Finland. As a result, people began to look for ways to protect the artifacts. President Theodore Roosevelt made Mesa Verde a National Park in 1906. He was assisted by work done by Virginia McClurg.

WHO WAS Virginia McClurg?

Virginia McClurg was a writer who lived from 1857 to 1931. She traveled to the Four Corners area on assignment for the New York Daily Graphic newspaper. She fell in love with what she called the "buried cities and lost homes" of the Ancestral Puebloans. She was determined to protect the place from vandalism and theft, so she traveled around the country telling people about the amazing finds at Mesa Verde. She organized people in support and enlisted the cooperation of the Native Americans who lived near by. Her work paved the way for President Roosevelt's declaration of Mesa Verde as a National Park.

Scientific excavations

By the time Dr. Jesse Walter Fewkes began systematic excavations of Mesa Verde, archaeology had become a respected profession, and techniques were improving. Fewkes was working for the Smithsonian Institution. He used techniques such as marking off the area in grids, mapping the location of finds, and cataloging artifacts. Tools such as shovels, trowels, and brushes were used. Care was taken to unearth artifacts without damaging them. Above-ground finds were also gathered. Some of the buildings needed care where stone walls had fallen. By 1917 Dr. Fewkes had started the first park museum. He paid attention to every detail, even noting the fibers used for clothing, bones, remains of fire pits, pottery, and bits of human skeletons.

Since then, work has continued at Mesa Verde and has expanded into the surrounding areas. Archaeologists look at old finds again using new technology to add to their understanding of the Ancestral Puebloan culture.

▷ *Teams of archaeologists worked to stabilize and preserve Balcony House in around 1910.*

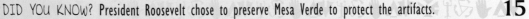

HOUSING

Mesa Verde is a land of dramatic contrasts. Fertile, moist land and abundant plant life carpets flat mesa tops above steep rock cliffs. A mesa is an elevated area of land that is flat like a table and which has at least one steep cliff on the side. Mesas are formed when erosion wears the surrounding area away. At lower levels tall trees such as pine and oak grow. Streams wander through ravines where cottonwoods and willows flourish. All this is surrounded by the dry deserts of the Southwest.

The dwellings at Mesa Verde are evidence of a culture that had adapted creatively to its surroundings. Built without the use of animals, wheeled vehicles, or modern tools, they are a wonder to people of today.

Archaeology Challenge

Pithouses are not very strong, so weather and time have demolished most of them. Archaeologists have found some of the shallow pits as they excavate, and this has allowed for them to be recreated for people to see how they would have looked then.

Living on the Mesa tops

Around the year C.E. 550, when the Ancestral Puebloans were settling in Mesa Verde, they were using a style of architecture called a pithouse. They dug out an area up to about 5 feet (1.5 meters) deep with a flat bottom. The sides of the pit were often finished with mud as plaster, or a stone façade. This underground living space was sheltered from sun and rain with a roof made of wooden poles, grasses, and branches. A final coating of mud for plaster helped to shield and insulate against extreme weather. The finished roof stood several feet above ground level. Inside was a place for keeping a fire, for warmth and cooking. There were open spaces incorporated into the design to let out the smoke from the fire.

Until about C.E. 700, the pithouses were usually round and anywhere from 9 to 25 feet (2.7 to 7.5 meters) across. An additional area was often dug out for storage with a stone slab used as a cover. Later pithouses were sometimes rectangles, squares, or "D" shaped. Eventually the Ancestral Puebloans began to build larger pit structures, called kivas, for gatherings. These could be as big as 40 feet (12 meters) across. A framework of beams was used to support the roof.

▷ *The dwellings at Mesa Verde have small windows to keep them warm in winter.*

First pueblos

Near the year C.E. 750, the people of Mesa Verde began to develop other architectural techniques using timber, mud, and stone. When this happened structures began to be built above ground, with rooms built upon rooms. These homes have been referred to as "pueblos," which is a Spanish word for "community" or "town dwellers."

These dwellings were elaborate and well constructed. Some of them had tunnels. They required cooperative work to assemble. Wooden frameworks were covered with adobe or mud. Doorways were small because the Ancestral Puebloans were not as large as most people today. The average height of a man was 5 feet 4 inches (1.6 meters).

Fantasy or Fact?

Spanish explorers heard stories of cities made of gold in the western United States. Though they did not find cities of gold, they did find beautiful cities made of clay and stone.

▷ *Mesa Verde Square Tower may have been used for observing the sky at night.*

Using stone

The people of Mesa Verde also learned how to carve the soft sandstone of the cliffs into blocks to use for building their pueblos. Spaces between blocks were filled with a mortar made of water, dirt, and ash. The gaps in the timber roofs were filled with stones and mortar. Rather than building many separate houses, the Ancestral Puebloan people learned to build an arrangement of rooms—like apartments in cities today.

Some areas in the multi-room dwellings were for cooking, other areas for sleeping, and certain areas were for gatherings or religious ceremonies. Families often had their own kiva, which was a place for religious ceremonies.

△ *Ladders were useful when you lived on a cliff.*

◁ *Caves provided a natural shelter for the Ancestral Puebloans.*

Moving into the cliffs

In the steep walls below the mesas were caves, formed through erosion. The Ancestral Puebloan people discovered them and eventually they moved into the cliffs and tucked their multi-room, several story high dwellings inside these caves. This happened around C.E. 1100 and continued until the people left Mesa Verde.

EYEWITNESS

"Strange and indescribable is the impression on the traveler, when, after a long and tiring ride through the boundless, monotonous **pinon** forest, he suddenly halts on the brink of the precipice, and in the opposite cliff beholds the ruins of the Cliff Palace ... This ruin well deserves its name, for with its round towers and high walls rising out of the heaps of stones ... it resembles at a distance an enchanted castle."

Gustaf Nordenskiöld

△ *Paintings decorated some walls inside the dwellings.*

Fantasy or Fact?

Some people think that the people of Mesa Verde moved into the cliffs for defense. They point out that these dwellings would be sheltered from enemy attack and were difficult to approach. Others say that a cave is not a good place to be in a time of war because the enemy can trap you inside. Another possible reason is that in a period of great climate changes, people may have needed shelter from colder than normal temperatures. Another explanation is that they wanted to remove their dwellings from the mesa top in order to leave that land available for more farming as their population grew. It is possible that they moved for a combination of these or other reasons.

Usually, the Ancestral Puebloans preferred to build in caves that faced south in order to soak up as much sun as possible for warmth in the colder months. They still climbed up to the mesa top for activities, such as farming. They used removable ladders and foot and handholds that they carved into the side of the mesa. They also had to climb down into the canyon and back up again with lumber, sandstone, river rocks, and clay—the materials needed for their homes, pottery, and tools. Particularly amazing is the fact that all of this was done with very simple, natural technology.

mortar

△ *The mortar used to hold the bricks together can still be seen today.*

◁ *T-shaped doorways in the Mesa Verde buildings have puzzled archaeologists. Some think that the design allowed in maximum light while cutting down on drafts. Also, the wider top allowed people to enter while carrying things.*

HUNTING, GATHERING, AND FARMING

The Ancestral Puebloan people's primary work was survival. Like their ancestors they hunted animals. For many years they used spears that were thrown with an atlatl. An atlatl is a piece of wood with a handgrip on one end and a notch that held a spear in the other. The atlatl works by adding more force and distance to the throw than could be achieved without it. Around the time that the Ancestral Puebloans arrived at Mesa Verde, they began to use bows and arrows. We know this because archaeologists have found both spears and bows and arrows at Mesa Verde, and they can determine their age using methods such as radiocarbon dating or stratigraphy.

The introduction of a new tool or craft can dramatically alter a civilization. In the case of the bow and arrow, hunters gained more accuracy and a longer range. Sinew or rope was strung onto a single piece of wood. Arrows were tipped with sharpened wood or stone points. The stone points were made from local rocks and minerals, such as quartz or flint. The Ancestral Puebloans hunted animals, such as deer, squirrels, and rabbits. Improved success with hunting helped them to stay well fed and healthy.

Archaeology Challenge

Stratigraphy is when archaeologists determine the age of an item by studying the depth of an artifact in the dig. As long as natural disaster or recent building has not disturbed the ground, it can be assumed that the deeper an item is buried, the older it is. Items found at equal depth are assumed to be of about the same age. Geologists can sometimes help in this process, by studying the layers of earth and offering ideas about what the rock and soil layers tell us about various time periods.

▷ *Arrows could have been used for hunting or for defense.*

Using plants

Traditionally Ancestral Puebloans also gathered plant foods such as berries, piñon nuts, and herbs. Piñon nuts were roasted or eaten raw. They could also be ground into flour. Honey was used to sweeten food. The Ancestral Puebloan people were very resourceful, using every part of the animal or plant. For example they would eat the fruit and flowers of the yucca plant. But they did not leave the rest of the plant unused. The roots could be made into a soapy lather for cleaning. They used the remaining fibers to weave sandals or make paintbrushes. The same thinking applied to animals. Deer provided hides, tendons to use like string, and antlers for scraping. The Ancestral Puebloans ate the meat and saved the bones for making tools.

▽ *Archaeologists have found corn cobs in Mesa Verde.*

The switch to farming

Just as the bow and arrow created changes in their lifestyle, so did other things. Around C.E. 550, the people of the Mesa Verde area became farmers, cultivating the fertile land where they settled. One of the most important crops was corn. Their corn grew on small ears in many colors. Corn was nourishing, versatile, and provided a foundation for their diet. They probably learned about this crop from their neighbors to the south.

Corn required a lot of work: preparing the land, planting, weeding and watering, harvesting, drying, grinding, and storing. Archaeologists have learned from studying the teeth of the Ancestral Puebloans that little bits of stone also got into the cornmeal, because the people's teeth were ground down. But corn enriched their diet, and it allowed them to create a settled community. They no longer had to migrate constantly in search of new sources of food. They also grew squash and beans. The highly nutritious beans, like corn, could be dried and stored for a long time. Turkeys also provided meat and eggs.

▽ *Bending over manos and metates to grind corn could cause sore joints and backache.*

manos

metates

New techniques

This ancient culture had some very advanced ideas about agriculture. For example they used terrace-style farming to make the most of the fertile land and varying altitudes. There is archaeological evidence of the people having created walls for reservoirs in order to conserve the sparse water for their crops. They still supplemented their diet by hunting and gathering. The success of their farming is even more remarkable considering that they had no metal tools, plows, work animals, or wheeled vehicles.

Archaeology Challenge

Archaeologists have found elk and deer bones in the older Mesa Verde area settlements, while new settlements have bones from smaller animals such as rabbits. This has made them consider the possibility that the reason the Ancestral Puebloans left Mesa Verde is that they were running out of large animals to hunt. If this were so, could this be because of over-hunting, or due to a lack of sufficient wild plants or crops to attract and feed a population of large animals?

◁ *Terraces are steps cut into a hillside to provide lots of small flat areas for farming, where there would otherwise be a slope. Archaeologists have found terraces at Mesa Verde.*

DAILY LIFE

Hunting, gathering, and farming took up much of the Ancestral Puebloans' time. In the remaining time, they ate, did chores, played, and developed their culture. Daily life revolved around family, community, and religious beliefs.

Religion

The Ancestral Puebloans believed in gods who governed their world and their lives. They also believed in the presence of spirits of their ancestors. As they lived their daily life, they were mindful of both gods and spirits and tried to live in a way that would be pleasing to them. They believed that they had to be good caretakers of the land, that it did not belong to them, and that all living things were linked together.

Their church was called a kiva, and in the middle of it was an opening called a sipapu. The sipapu was a reminder of the spirit world that they came from and to which they would return someday. They believed that somewhere on Earth was an opening for spirits, perhaps where a natural formation indicated a break in Earth's surface. This opening might be in a canyon or beneath a stream. The opening in their kiva was symbolic of that opening, or sipapu.

sipapu

△ *The sipapu in the kiva held great symbolic meaning for the Ancestral Puebloans.*

Family and community

The relationships between people are one of the areas that archaeologists find hardest to describe. The artifacts simply do not reveal answers to all of our questions. This is where archaeologists can rely upon information from anthropologists and from the living descendants of the people they are studying.

Modern Puebloan people, such as the Hopi, are traditionally matrilineal, which means that they belong to clans according to who their mother is. When a man marries a woman, he generally moves into the household of his bride. Women hold a higher status in some areas, such as land ownership. Men, however, have certain roles reserved for them. For instance, the village chiefs are usually men.

Archaeology Challenge

Were there rich and poor people in Ancestral Puebloan society? Archaeologists look for clues about wealth and status by noting the quantity and quality of items buried with people and the size or design of dwellings. In the case of the Ancestral Puebloans, there have been very few examples of personal wealth or power, making it likely that their society was very equal. But, toward the end of their stay at Mesa Verde, they may have begun to place individuals in positions of great responsibility, such as distributor of crop surpluses.

▷ *Petroglyphs carved by Ancestral Puebloans often show people and scenes of daily life at Mesa Verde.*

Children

Artifacts help us to learn what it was like to be a child living in Mesa Verde. Small dolls in cradles and miniature arrows have been found. Children would also help with chores and learn to make baskets and pottery, tools, and weapons. There was also time for fun. Children may have played a game with a hoop and stick or used rattles for play and music. Rattles could be made from dried gourds filled with seeds. Some children probably had dogs as pets and companions.

Food and clothing

Obtaining, preparing, storing, and eating food took up a great deal of time and energy for the inhabitants of Mesa Verde. Hunting, gathering, farming, and perhaps sometimes trading provided them with a variety of foods such as meat, pumpkin, beans, corn, berries, seeds, and nuts. Meats were roasted, stewed, or dried as jerky. Jerky lasted a lot longer than fresh meat.

Archaeology Challenge

When archaeologists find things they have to be careful with their guesswork. What might look like a toy doll to them, based on their own present-day culture, could actually be an item used to represent a god or could have a ceremonial purpose. The descendants of the Ancestral Puebloans, such as the Hopi and Zuni people, can often explain what an item is used for.

Preparing food

Preparing food could be difficult work, requiring husking, shelling, cooking, drying, and sometimes grinding. Corn was dried and stored on the cob. It was also ground into cornmeal. It was probably cooked on a hot greased rock in the way that we cook pancakes on skillets. Strips of squash were hung to dry. Nuts and seeds were shelled and dried before eating.

Archaeology Challenge

When archaeologists find a bone, how do they know whether it was from an animal used for food or just a wild animal that died at the site? One way is to look for evidence of charring, which would show that the animal was cooked.

Garbage

Prehistoric garbage heaps contain treasures for archaeologists. These piles of discarded bones, broken pottery, and other items are a virtual timeline for scientific study. Layer upon layer tells about the people who lived there. The types of bones can reveal what kind of meat the people were eating. Also, cooking tools and vessels say much about how they prepared their food.

garbage heap

Making pottery

Learning to make pottery was a major, civilization-changing development. Clay jars were used for storage and cooking. Unlike baskets clay pots could be placed on or near a fire. This was a new and more efficient cooking technique. Soot-blackened walls are lasting evidence of these fires, which cooked food and kept families warm.

▷ *Food that had been hunted, gathered, or farmed was cooked in pots like this one.*

Fire

Hearth fires that burned long ago also leave clues about the Ancestral Puebloan people. When the hearth was hot, iron particles in the clay the hearth was made of were able to move around. Earth's magnetism caused them to point directly at the magnetic north pole. Years after the last fire has burnt out, the iron particles are still frozen in the same position they were in the last time the clay was heated. Scientists have noticed that Earth's magnetic north varies because the Earth moves in relation to other heavenly bodies. By studying the iron particles of old hearth sites, scientists can determine where magnetic north was at that time and therefore establish a date for the last fire in the hearth.

burn marks

hearth

▷ *Fire was important to life at Mesa Verde. Most of the buildings contain hearths, like this one.*

Clothing

Cloth garments have not been well preserved, but archaeologists believe that the men wore loincloths and women some type of small apron. Sandals were woven of yucca fibers, and they even made socks using yucca and feathers. Leather moccasins have been found, but are rare. In cold weather robes or blankets of fibers, feathers, and fur helped to keep them warm. They may have used snowshoes as well.

War

When the Ancestral Puebloan people first began settling in the Mesa Verde area, their pithouses were scattered and easily visible. Because they were not together or hidden, it seems they were relatively free of warfare. But there is evidence that defending themselves against war may have become a large part of their lives toward the end of their stay at Mesa Verde. Some buildings appear to have been altered to make them more secure. The condition of some skeletons found in the area suggested a violent death and the clustering of dwellings inside the cliff has been used to support theories of warfare. Also, rock art found near Mesa Verde has pictures of people with bows, arrows, and shields engaged in combat.

▷ *Necklaces have been found at Mesa Verde. They show that some Ancestral Puebloan clothing was decorative, rather than practical.*

ARTS AND CRAFTS

Artistic expression was important to the people of Mesa Verde. They placed designs that were beautiful and symbolic of their beliefs onto everyday objects. They created jewelry for its beauty and kachina dolls (see p. 40) for worship. They made musical instruments from bones. They used walls of rock to draw their stories on.

Rock art

The Ancestral Puebloan people created many pictures on rock. Pictographs were painted with natural dyes and paintbrushes created from frayed plant stems. Petroglyphs were done by etching—scraping into the rock with hard tools. Images of hands may have been used as a signature. The Ancestral Puebloan people left no words recording their history. But pictures were used to communicate meaning before words. The artwork may illustrate the history of their community. The pictographs and petroglyphs could have strong religious significance. Some appear to be telling creation stories.

Baskets

Long before they began to make pottery, the Ancestral Puebloans made baskets. Baskets were made using split willow and other plant materials. They used spiraled coils and weaving techniques to create baskets for many purposes. Beautiful geometric patterns were often woven into the baskets.

△ *Some beautifully decorated pottery has survived in one piece.*

Pottery

The skill of pottery making was probably learned from people who lived south of Mesa Verde. Pottery was not just for cooking—it also offered a new creative outlet. Using natural materials they fashioned vessels that were useful and beautiful. When archaeologists study a piece of pottery, they can often tell what culture it is from because of particular designs, styles, and symbols.

Pottery techniques

Ancestral Puebloan pottery was made by gathering clay from the ground. The Ancestral Puebloans learned just how much water to add to the clay to make it workable, but still strong. Slip was made using clay and water and was used to join pieces together, like a handle attached to a mug. They shaped their pots by starting with coils that were built one upon the other. They were smoothed by hand or by using a tool.

Pots could be decorated with paints made by boiling minerals or plants in water. They were applied by using brushes made of fur or plant materials. They fired their pots by starting wood fires in trenches designed for just the right airflow.

▽ *Fingerprints and fingernail marks are a lasting record of the human hands that shaped each vessel.*

Learning from pottery

Pottery preserves well and is fairly easy to date, so archaeologists often study it. Pottery is found abundantly at Mesa Verde—one building has even been named Mug House because of the many mugs that were found there. Archaeologists have also found many bowls, ladles, jars, and other pottery items lying in and around the pueblo homes. Shards, which are broken pieces, are found scattered underfoot like stones in some areas.

Pottery is a useful type of object to study because it tells about culture, religion, and daily life. From pottery we can learn about diet, habits, population, trade, family, and social structure. When archaeologists study a piece of pottery, they can learn about where the clay came from depending on what substances are in it. Once pottery is dated, the items near it can also be dated.

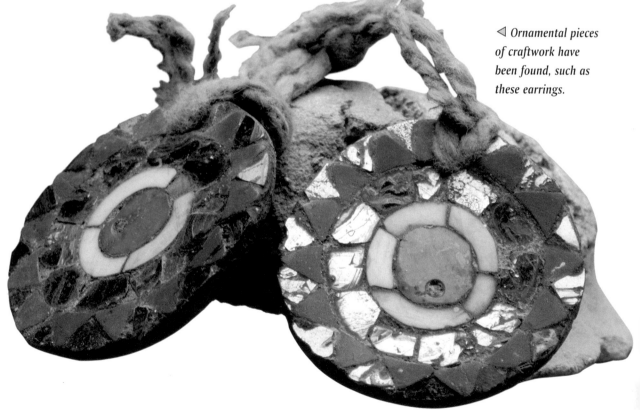

◁ *Ornamental pieces of craftwork have been found, such as these earrings.*

Weaving and sewing

The Ancestral Puebloans spun cotton into yarn using a spindle. They wove the yarn with other fibers and feathers using a loom. They became skillful weavers who could make a variety of clothing items. They also used sharp awls to pierce leather for sewing and created sewing needles with animal bones. Robes could be made of fur. Since the materials used for clothing do not preserve well, we have very few examples of their original garments. But the Puebloan people of today continue to create traditional weavings that give us an idea of what the Ancestral Puebloans must have worn.

Archaeology Challenge

There were hooks on the walls at Mesa Verde. But what the people used them for was a mystery. Then, archaeologists talked to the modern Puebloan people who are descended from the Ancestral Puebloans. They do a lot of beautiful weaving and they hang their looms from similar wall hooks.

TRAVEL AND TRADE

The Ancestral Puebloan people of the Mesa Verde region were not isolated from other groups of people. We know this because objects found there had to come from other areas. For instance small pieces of cotton garments have been found. Cotton cannot be grown at Mesa Verde because of the climate, so this was probably obtained through a southern trade route. Likewise seashells from California have been discovered along with parrot feathers and copper bells believed to have come from Mexico. Turquoise jewelry was probably obtained by trade as well.

There are different types of trade. The Ancestral Puebloans probably traded within their own community. A person who was especially gifted at making spear points might trade those in exchange for someone else's baskets. In this way work became specialized. Trade also would occur with nearby neighbors.

Goods could eventually be passed across great distances, going just from one village to the next. This would be a practical way of obtaining new and exotic items from far away during a time when people traveled on foot.

▷*Socks like this would have been especially useful to traders, who had to travel very long distances in cold weather.*

Trade would create a network of communities that depended on each other. It also suggests an organized and advanced society. There may have also been some long distance travel, but it would take a very long time. They did not have horses or wheeled vehicles, and they had to carry all their belongings on their back.

There is a great deal of interest in the Chaco Canyon area of New Mexico, which is near Mesa Verde. It appears that the culture there was flourishing around the same time that activity at Mesa Verde was at its peak. It seems that Chaco Canyon could have been a bustling center of trade from about the 9th century C.E. to the 12th century C.E. This theory has arisen because there are a number of buildings of several types, and also huge amounts of some goods such as turquoise.

Archaeology Challenge

Archaeologists have found paths leading out from Chaco Canyon, like spokes of a wheel. Some scientists think that the roads are merely small footpaths. But modern technology makes it possible to get a better look. Aerial surveys examine roads from the air, so that the most important routes can be worked out. These surveys show that marker rocks were deliberately placed to draw attention to or maintain the path.

▽ *The finds that archaeologists have made at Chaco Canyon have told them more about life at Mesa Verde.*

ABANDONING THE CLIFFS

The people of Mesa Verde appear to have left their homes in a fairly short span of time around C.E. 1300. How does archaeology tell us this? What does it say about why they left and where they went? Those who study the Ancestral Puebloans have wondered what reason could have been powerful enough to cause the society to abandon buildings that they had worked hard on for a long time. They left some buildings unfinished, as though the move was decided upon suddenly.

The end of Mesa Verde

Over the years archaeologists have developed many theories about why the Ancestral Puebloans left Mesa Verde. Each new discovery brings us closer to finding the truth.

Warfare

Warfare may have been a part of the reason for leaving. There is evidence of warfare at Mesa Verde. Some skeletal remains show that death was caused by violence. Some weapons have been preserved.

The architecture at Mesa Verde also appears to have features designed for defense.

▷ *Once a whole family would have lived in this dwelling. Then they suddenly disappeared. Archaeologists are still not sure of the reasons why.*

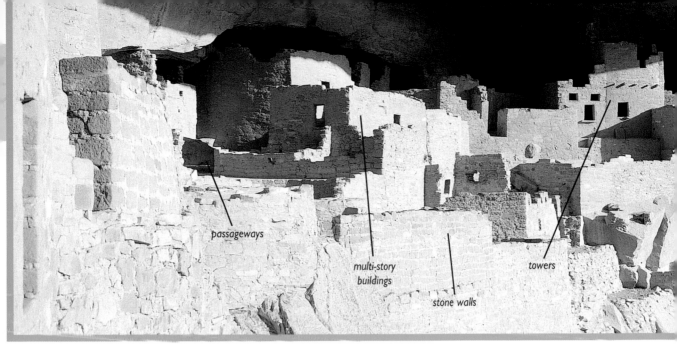

passageways

multi-story buildings

towers

stone walls

△ *The defensive features of the dwellings at Cliff Palace suggest that battles may have been fought.*

Walls, multi-story buildings, secure and difficult-to-enter passageways, and towers could all have had defense purposes. But towers that were thought to be used for defense may have had a religious significance instead, or might have been used as observation places for viewing the sky.

Often burnt buildings show evidence of war. These are present at Mesa Verde as well. But some of the buildings do not seem to have been burnt through to the beams. So archaeologists are not sure that a wartime siege is the right explanation. There is not any clear cut evidence of an enemy. For instance, if an enemy drove them from their homes, why did the enemy not remain after they drove everyone else away?

Also, while some people point to the cliff-dwellings as evidence of a society that was trying to cluster and stay in positions with natural defenses, there are others who point out that the Ancestral Puebloans may have simply moved into the cliffs to leave more room on the fertile mesa top for farming.

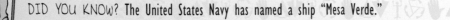

Drought

For a long time people believed that drought was the main reason why the people of Mesa Verde left. It was a reasonable conclusion from the archaeological evidence. Tree rings indicated a twenty-year drought around the time of their departure. A drought would have made farming difficult and drinking water scarce. Without any other strong evidence, this seemed like a reasonable explanation.

◁ *Kachina dolls may have had a religious purpose.*

Further research indicated that some long droughts also occurred at other times when the Ancestral Puebloans stayed. Some people believe that it would have taken more than a drought to make the people want to leave. Others think that drought would be reason enough, especially if it lasted longer or was more severe than in previous years.

Other theories

There are many other possible solutions, including climate changes, not enough resources, such as food, for a growing population, and religious divisions. Some think a new religion pulled the people into southern regions. Some may have moved to other groups. The similarity of them to the Puebloan people of today suggests a connection. However the absence of certain architectural elements, such as the towers that had been built at Mesa Verde, suggests a new way of life that caused them to leave certain aspects of their culture behind.

What really happened?

Perhaps the best theory is that the Ancestral Puebloan people left due to a combination of factors. For instance the drought may not only have made it hard to farm, but also shaken their faith, causing them to look to another group's beliefs for blessings for their crops. They may also have been finding wild animals scarcer or struggling with less fertile land. Combined with an increasing population, tensions could have been high, and there may have been some battles. Perhaps a series of frustrations pushed the people to move away?

Where did they go?

No matter why they left, the story of the Ancestral Puebloan people of Mesa Verde does not end with their departure. Their history is ingrained in the Puebloan people of today who believe that they are connected to these and other inhabitants of the American Southwest.

△ *Modern day Puebloan people are believed to have descended from the Ancestral Puebloans.*

MESA VERDE ARCHAEOLOGY TODAY

Mesa Verde became a national park in 1906, and the land and artifacts are protected by law. Through the care of many individuals and organizations, the story of ancient people has been preserved. This is not always an easy task.

Natural dangers

The same forces of nature that carved the mesas also affect the architecture of the Ancestral Puebloans. In November of 1995, seeping water was discovered at Cliff Palace. Park staff and volunteers had to bail Cliff Palace out using buckets to ladle away water and ice. This type of care helps to guarantee a future for the artifacts of Mesa Verde.

Water is not the only natural force that has been a problem—fire is also a big concern. In recent years there have been five large wildfires at Mesa Verde. Lightning strikes and dry conditions are the two main causes of wildfires. People are working to reduce the quantity of dry plant material and to develop other strategies for preventing and fighting fires in the region, as well as protecting people and artifacts.

▷ *Archaeologists have continued to study the area since it was first discovered.*

Legal protection

Laws have been enacted to guard the artifacts from damage and theft. Archaeologists leave some artifacts undisturbed. They do this because they know that future scientists will have more advanced methods for studying them. As artifacts are reconsidered in the light of new knowledge, many old ideas about the people of Mesa Verde are challenged.

Learning at Mesa Verde

It is not just archaeologists who learn from Mesa Verde. Students and park visitors also gain an increased understanding of the Ancestral Puebloans. In addition to visiting Mesa Verde, museums have exhibits where people can learn more about the Ancestral Puebloans.

An interesting way to study the people of Mesa Verde is to try to live as they did, by trying to build a pithouse, weave a basket, or shape a bowl from clay. Special programs such as these have been conducted for school groups and tourists of the Mesa Verde area.

The Four Corners area has a rich concentration of archaeological sites. Many artifacts of the Ancestral Puebloans lie outside of the national park, on reservations and other private land. There are still many unanswered questions and many opportunities for exciting new discoveries about the prehistoric people of Mesa Verde. Mesa Verde is more than just a fascinating tourist attraction to many people. To the native people who trace their ancestry to the amazing Pueblo villages of Mesa Verde, it is a beloved place.

Approx. 33000 B.C.E.–18000 B.C.E.

People come to North America from Asia, across the Bering Strait land bridge. They gradually disperse across North and South America. They are primarily hunter-gatherers and travel from place to place.

Approx. C.E. 550

The Ancestral Puebloans, also called the Basketmakers, settle at Mesa Verde and in surrounding areas. Their nomadic lifestyle ends and they begin to live in small villages of pithouses. They still make baskets, but are beginning to learn techniques for making pottery. They introduce bows and arrows for hunting, and they start to grow corn and other crops.

Approx. C.E. 700– 900

The Ancestral Puebloans develop their culture, making more pottery. They also begin to improve their houses by building them above ground in a Pueblo style, sometimes with blocks of sandstone.

Approx. C.E. 900–1150

In the nearby Chaco Canyon region, culture is flourishing. The culture there is linked to the Mesa Verde region by trade routes. At Mesa Verde, multi-story buildings are developed with kivas.

Approx. C.E. 1100–1300

This is known as the Classic or Great Pueblo period at Mesa Verde. The Ancestral Puebloans build larger, more complex homes and move into the cliffs. They continue to create elaborate pottery. By this point they have developed a complex society where responsibilities are divided among members of the community. Many people specialize in certain types of work, based on their skills, and trade by bartering.

Approx. C.E. 1211–1278

Spruce Tree House is built at Mesa Verde.

C.E. 1276

A long period of drought begins in the Mesa Verde area.

By C.E. 1300

The dwellings at Mesa Verde are abandoned. The Ancestral Puebloans have dispersed east to the Rio Grande and off to the lands of the Hopi and the Zuni.

Today

Modern Pueblo groups such as the Hopi and Zuni still live in the Four Corners area. Although modern in many ways, they still carry on some of the traditions of the Ancestral Puebloans.

Approx. C.E. 1300-1800s

The dwellings at Mesa Verde are empty. Native peoples from the surrounding areas probably see the dwellings, but do not disturb them.

1859

Professor J. S. Newberry explores the area and makes the first known reference to "Mesa Verde" in his report. He does not mention seeing any cliff dwellings, so he probably did not explore much of the area.

1874

Two-story Cliff House is discovered by W. H. Jackson. It is the first dwelling in Mesa Verde known to have been entered by white men.

1875

Sixteen Window House is discovered by W. H. Holmes on a government survey expedition.

1884

A prospector named S. E. Osborn enters Balcony House.

1886

Chief Acowitz tells Richard Wetherill about the houses of "The Ancient Ones."

1888

Richard Wetherill and his brother-in-law Charles Mason find Cliff Palace while looking for their cattle. Wetherill's brother Al saw Cliff Palace from a distance the year before, but he did not enter it.

1889

Wetherill and some of his brothers begin to explore the dwellings at Cliff Palace.

By 1890

Richard Wetherill and his brothers have located about 200 Mesa Verde dwellings.

1891

A Swedish professor, Gustaf Nordenskiöld, visits Mesa Verde. He is the the first scientist to study Mesa Verde.

1893

Nordenskiöld publishes a book about Mesa Verde.

1901

A bill is introduced to Congress to make Mesa Verde a national park, but it does not pass.

1906

A bill to make Mesa Verde a national park is finally passed by Congress, and President Theodore Roosevelt signs it on June 29. Mesa Verde National Park is the first and only national park created for the preservation of the work of human hands. Also in 1906 the Antiquities Act is passed. This makes it a crime to collect or destroy artifacts found on federal land.

1908

James Garfield, Secretary of the Interior, appoints ethnologist/archaeologist Dr. Jesse Walter Fewkes, of the Smithsonian Institution, to oversee the excavation and maintenance of Mesa Verde. Excavation and repair of major sites begins, so that visitors can see the site.

1917

Mesa Verde National Park Museum is founded by Dr. Fewkes.

1959–1972

The Wetherill Archaeological Project excavates Mug House, Long House and Step House, as well as three mesa top sites.

1978

UNESCO declares Mesa Verde to be a World Cultural Heritage Site.

Currently

Research and preservation continue. Educational programs are offered for tourists and students.

GLOSSARY

aesthetic
relating to sense of art or beauty

altitude
another word meaning height

ancestor
distant relative from whom one is descended

anthropologist
scientist who studies the development of the human species and cultures

arid
dry

artifact
object made by people, such as a tool or an ornament. Archaeologists often use the word "artifacts" to describe the objects they find that were made by people in past times.

awl
small tool with a sharp point

bartering
exchange or trade goods without using money

clan
group of families with the same surname, led by a chief

descendants
sons, daughters, grandchildren, or their children

dwelling
somewhere people live

edible
good for eating

erosion
process of being worn away over time, often by the weather

ethical
what is morally right

excavate
dig up a building or area of land in order to look for ancient objects, ruins, or other evidence from the past

façade
outer surface

fertile
soil that is good for growing crops

flint
hard stone flaked to form a primitive tool or weapon

glacier
huge mass of ice, created when snow falls year after year, but does not melt

gourd
similar to a squash or melon. Can be dried and used as a tool, vessel, or musical instrument.

habitat
particular environment

Hopi
group of Pueblo Indians, living primarily in Arizona. Their name has been translated to mean "peaceful ones."

insulate
use a material to stop heat escaping

kachina
one of the spirits in Ancestral Puebloan mythology

linguist
person who studies the invention and development of language

loom
device for weaving

mano
stone held in the hand and used with a metate for grinding food, such as corn

matrilineal
following the female line in a family

mesa
flat-topped, high piece of land with steep sides

metate
curved stone that holds things that are ground with a mano

migrate
travel in search of a new place to live, often as part of a large group of migrating people

mortar
mixture made to hold stones together and fill cracks

nomadic
lifestyle in which people are always moving, not settling in one area for very long

parch
to heat and dry

petroglyph
rock-carving

pictograph
writing using picture symbols instead of letters

piñon
type of pine tree, or pine nut

plateau
area of high, flat land

prehistoric
occuring before recorded history

Quaker
name for person who belongs to religious group called The Society of Friends

radiocarbon dating
way of discovering the age of some objects by measuring the amount of substance, called carbon, that they contain. It works because plants and animals absorb a special type of carbon, Carbon-14, from the air when they are alive. When they die, this carbon disappears at a known rate. So the amount present in a piece of wood, bone, or other material that was once a part of a plant or animal reveals how old the material is

reservoirs
areas that store water

siege
surround a place, not allowing anyone to leave or enter, in order to capture it

sinew
tendon

slip
combination of clay and water used to join pieces of pottery

spindle
thin rod used to hold, twist, or wind a fiber used in knitting or weaving

symbolic
image or gesture used to represent a belief or idea

symmetrical
balanced design

terrace-style farming
using multi-level fields or gardens to make the most of rainfall for crops

timber
wood used in building

tuberculosis
contagious disease of the lungs

Ute
native people who have lived in Colorado longer than any other group. Utah is named after them, and there are many Ancestral Puebloan ruins there.

vessel
container for liquids

yucca
flowering desert plant with stiff and pointed leaves

Zuni
Pueblo people of New Mexico

FURTHER READING

Arnold, Caroline. *Ancient Cliff Dwellers of Mesa Verde*. Minneapolis: Sagebrush, 2001.

Peterson, David. *Mesa Verde National Park*. USA: Children's Press, 1992.

Shuter, Jane. *Mesa Verde*. Chicago: Heinemann Library: 2000.